W9-AJP-626

The Emperor's New Clothes

Retold by Robina Beckles Willson
Illustrated by Doug Roy

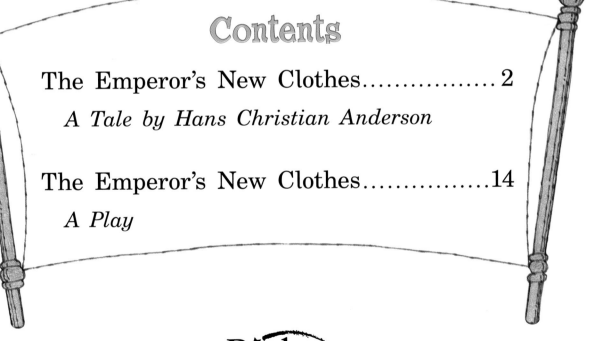

Contents

Rigby
A Harcourt Achieve Imprint

www.Rigby.com
1-800-531-5015

Many years ago, two women named Meg and Peg wanted to make money, but they did not want to work very hard to get it.

One day Meg said, "Our emperor spends a lot of money on clothes."

"I wish we could sell some clothes to him," said Peg.

"Maybe we could," said Meg. " I have a plan."

The next morning, Meg and Peg went to the emperor's huge palace. "We want to see the chief minister," said Meg to the guards.

The chief minister met Meg and Peg in the hall of the palace.

"We would like to see the emperor," said Meg and Peg.

"The emperor is too busy changing his clothes," explained the minister.

"We are the finest weavers in the world, and the emperor would be very upset if he found out you refused to let us in," said Meg.

The minister agreed, and a few minutes later the emperor appeared.

2ND FLOOR • Emperor's 400 Closets

1ST FLOOR • Emperor's 100 Bedrooms

GROUND FLOOR • Kitchen, Throne & Government

BASEMENT • Dungeons

"What did you two weavers bring to show me?" asked the emperor.

"Well, if you give us some money to buy some golden silk thread, we will weave the finest cloth for you," said Meg.

"Our cloth will tell you who is foolish because it can't be seen by people who are foolish," said Peg.

The emperor thought it might be quite
useful to have a cloth that told him who was
foolish, so he gave Meg and Peg lots
of money.

Meg and Peg hid the money and then set up the loom and began to weave. The next day the emperor's minister went to see the cloth. "Umm . . . it's beautiful," he said, even though he didn't see a stitch anywhere. He didn't want to seem foolish by saying he could not see the cloth.

Soon after, the emperor went to watch the weavers. He, too, pretended he could see the cloth because he didn't want to seem foolish.

The emperor ordered Meg and Peg to make a suit for him to wear in a parade the next day. The following morning, the emperor tried on his new suit. Meg and Peg told him how wonderful he looked.

During the parade, no one dared to say that they could not see the emperor's new suit. Suddenly, a small girl shouted, "Look, Mom! The emperor is in his underwear."

Peg, Meg, and the chief minister tried to hush the girl up, but the emperor had heard every word. Then he heard his people start to giggle and point. They were all saying that he had nothing on but his underwear.

The emperor realized he had been tricked. He wanted to hide, but he had to keep walking. He felt very cold and very foolish.

The End

The Emperor's New Clothes: A Play

The Characters

The Narrator

The Emperor

A Small Girl

Peg and Meg   The Minister   15

Scene 1

Peg and Meg are sitting on a street in a town, doing nothing.

Narrator: Many years ago, two women named Meg and Peg wanted to make money. However, they did not want to work very hard to get it.

**Meg:** Our emperor spends a lot of money on clothes.

**Peg:** I wish we could sell him some clothes.

Meg: Maybe we could. I have a plan.

**Narrator:** The next morning, Meg and Peg went to the emperor's huge palace.

Scene 2

At the doors of the emperor's palace. Two guards are standing by the doors. Peg and Meg arrive. They are talking to the minister.

 **Meg and Peg:** Chief minister, we would like to see the emperor.

 Minister: You can't. The emperor is busy changing his clothes. You must leave the palace now.

 **Meg:** We are the finest weavers in the world. The emperor would be very upset if he found out you wouldn't let us see him.

 **Narrator:** The minister did not want to upset the emperor so he let Meg and Peg wait. A few minutes later the emperor appeared.

 **Emperor:** What do you two weavers want to show me?

Meg: Nothing right now, but if you give us some money, we will buy some golden silk thread. Then we will weave the finest cloth for you.

Peg: The cloth will tell you who is foolish, because people who are foolish won't be able to see it.

Narrator: The emperor thought it might be very useful to have cloth that told him who was foolish, so he gave Meg and Peg lots of money.

Scene 3

Inside Peg and Meg's workshop.

Narrator: Meg and Peg hid the money. Then Meg set up the loom and pretended to weave. Soon after, the emperor and minister came to see the cloth. Of course, they didn't see any cloth, but they did not want to seem foolish. They pretended they did see it.

Emperor: I see the cloth and it is very lovely. I order you to make me a suit to wear in the parade tomorrow.

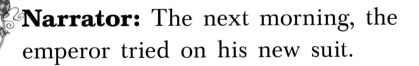

Narrator: The next morning, the
emperor tried on his new suit.

Meg and Peg: You look wonderful!

Scene 4

The parade through town. The emperor is walking along, wearing only his underwear.

**Narrator:** The emperor was at the head of the parade. Everyone said that his new clothes were beautiful. No one dared to say that they could not see the emperor's new suit. Suddenly, a small girl cried out.

Girl: Look, mom! The emperor is in his underwear.

Meg, Peg, and Minister: Shhhhhh!

Girl: But Mom, he's wearing only his underwear!

Meg, Peg, and Minister: Shhhhhh!

 **Narrator:** The emperor had heard the girl. Then he heard everyone giggle and say that he did only have his underwear on. All he could do was keep walking and try to hold his head high. He felt very cold and very foolish.

The End